THE FIFTY-MINUTE SUPERVISOR

2nd EDITION

Elwood N. Chapman

DISCARDED

CRISP PUBLICATIONS, INC.
Los Altos, California

THE FIFTY-MINUTE SUPERVISOR
SUPERVISOR
2nd Edition

by Elwood N. Chapman

CREDITS
Editor: **Michael G. Crisp**
Designer: **Carol Harris**
Typesetting: **Interface Studio**
Cover Design: **Carol Harris**

Copyright © 1986, 1988 by Crisp Publications, Inc.
Printed in the United States of America

Library of Congress Cataloging in Publication Data
Chapman, Elwood N.
The Fifty Minute Supervisor: 2nd Edition
L.C. number 85-72734
ISBN O-931961-58-0

PREFACE

Improving the quality of first line supervision has always been considered essential by successful executives because of the immediate impact on employee productivity. As a result, training directors allocate a sizable portion of their budget to new supervisor training. A common problem however, has been that considerable time may elapse between the time a new supervisor is promoted and before any training is provided. This can lead to costly mistakes or the formation of poor habits before formal training takes place. THE FIFTY-MINUTE SUPERVISOR was developed to remedy this ''training delay'' problem.

THE FIFTY-MINUTE SUPERVISOR should be considered Phase I of any training program. It was designed to be given to a new supervisor or an acting supervisor as soon as practical following promotion. All that is required is a pencil, a chair and some time. Once completed this program should help a new supervisor get off to a successful start. Later, following an ''on the job adjustment'' period, the individual will be better prepared for Phase II — a more formal supervisory training program.

Other Fifty-Minute self-study management training books that would be helpful to a new supervisor are listed on page 58.

ABOUT THIS BOOK

THE FIFTY-MINUTE SUPERVISOR is not like most books. It has a unique ''self-paced'' format that encourages a reader to become personally involved. Designed to be ''read with a pencil'', there are an abundance of exercises, activities, assessments and cases that invite participation.

The objective of THE FIFTY-MINUTE SUPERVISOR is to help a person recognize the traits that lead to successful supervision; and then make any required behavioral changes that apply the concepts presented in the book.

THE FIFTY-MINUTE SUPERVISOR (and the other self-improvement books listed on page 57) can be used effectively in a number of ways. Here are some possibilities:

— **Individual Study.** Because the book is self-instructional, it can be provided at the point of promotion. By completing the activities and exercises, a person should not only receive valuable feedback, but also practical ideas about steps for self-improvement.

— **Workshops and Seminars.** The book is ideal for pre-assigned reading prior to a workshop or seminar. With the basics in hand, the quality of the participation should improve. More time can be spent on concept extensions and applications during the program. The book can also be effective when a trainer distributes it at the beginning of a session, and leads participants through the contents.

— **Remote Location Training.** Copies can be sent to those not able to attend ''home office'' training sessions.

— **Informal Study Groups.** Thanks to the format, brevity and low cost, this book is ideal for ''brown-bag'' or other informal group sessions.

There are other possibilities that depend on the objectives, program or ideas or the user. One thing for sure, even after it has been read, this book will serve as excellent reference material which can be easily reviewed. Good luck!

TO THE READER

Congratulations on becoming a supervisor. After completing this brief book you will know many secrets of good supervision. What you learn, and any positive changes you make in your behavior, are far more important than the time it takes to finish, so please *do not read so fast that you miss something.*

To fully benefit, be honest, especially when you rate yourself on factors such as attitude and self-confidence. It is not what you are now, but what you can become as a successful supervisor that will help you progress in your organization. Good luck in your new venture.

Elwood N. Chapman

Elwood N. Chapman

P.S. The person who gave you this, believes in your future. If you have a problem as you proceed, please return to this individual for assistance. Keep this guide as a resource and refer to it on a regular basis as you make your transition into management.

Many new, inexperienced supervisors enjoy setting "success goals" for themselves. A good way to do this is to identify, discuss, and refine such goals with your immediate superior and then ask this person to monitor your progress for a thirty day period. If you wish, you can formalize this process by using the Voluntary Contract on the opposite page. One advantage in using the agreement is that your superior will recognize your sincerity and set a firm date for a review. Using the contract approach is a form of self-motivation.

VOLUNTARY
CONTRACT

I, _____ , hereby agree

(Your name)

to meet with the individual designated below within

thirty days to discuss my progress toward incorporating

the techniques and ideas presented in this supervisory

training program. The purpose of this meeting will be

to *review* areas of strength and establish action steps for

areas where improvement may still be required.

_____

Signature

I agree to meet with the above employee on,

_____

Month   *Date*   *Time*

at the following location.

_____

_____

Signature

CONTENTS

As you contemplate making your transition into a supervisory role, it is often a good idea to model your behavior after a successful supervisor you respect.

You will discover that the highly successful supervisors have much in common. If the opportunity presents itself, discuss some of the characteristics and principles of good supervision with your manager. Some of these characteristics are presented on the next page.

JUST DO IT!

MAKE YOUR CHOICE NOW

SUCCESSFUL SUPERVISORS	FAILURES

SUCCESSFUL SUPERVISORS

Supervisors who remain positive under stress.

Those who take time to teach employees what they know.

Those who build and maintain mutually rewarding relationships with their employees.

Supervisors who learn to set reasonable and consistant authority lines.

Those who learn to delegate.

Those who establish standards of high quality and set good examples.

Individuals who work hard to become good communicators.

Leaders who build team effort to achieve high productivity.

FAILURES

Supervisors who permit problems to get them down.

Those who rush instructions to employees and then fail to follow up.

Individuals insensitive to employee needs.

Those not interested in learning the basic supervisory skills.

Those who fail to understand it is not what a supervisor can do but what supervisors can get others to accomplish.

Supervisors who let their status go to their heads.

Those who become either too authoritarian or too lax.

Add your own:

_____   _____

_____   _____

_____   _____

As an employee, you have had the opportunity to study mistakes supervisors make. List three you do not intend to make.

1. _____

2. _____

3. _____

4

A case study is designed to provide insights you may not possess. Five case problems are included in this program. Please give them your careful attention.

The case on the opposite page will help you understand some of the things involved in making the transition to a successful supervisor. You can benefit from expressing your views and comparing them with those of the author.

CASE 1

WHO WILL SURVIVE?

Please assume that Joe and Mary are equally qualified to assume the role of supervisor in the same department. Further assume they adopt different attitudes toward their new challenge. Which one, in your opinion, stands the best chance of surviving after six months?

Joe received news of his promotion by throwing a party. The following day he made a list of do's and don'ts he would follow. Joe figured he had worked under enough supervisors to know what to do. He would model his behavior on what he had learned from observation. Why bother to study techniques and principles in advance? Why get needlessly uptight by too much preparation. Joe believes personality and good common sense is all that is needed. His strategy will be to set a good example by personally working hard, staying close to the group, and doing a lot of listening and concentrate on building good relationships in all directions. Joe has complete confidence in his ability to succeed.

Mary was delighted with the announcement of her promotion. She decided to use the two week period to prepare for her new responsibilities. She quickly found some good books on supervision and started to make a list of recommended techniques to follow. How to demonstrate authority? When to delegate? What changes in behavior would be required, etc.? Mary accepted the premise that she had much to learn about becoming a successful supervisor. Although she believes in herself, she does not have Joe's level of confidence. Mary has decided on the following strategy. Although she intends to remain friendly and upbeat, she will slowly pull back from too much personal contact with former fellow-employees. She feels this will be necessary to demonstrate her authority. Next she will concentrate on creating a good working environment so that workers are more relaxed. Everything will be planned and orderly. Everyone will know where he/she stand and what is expected.

Which individual has the better chance of survival? Will Joe with his upbeat, confident approach do a better job than Mary with her more scientific attitude? Or will Mary, with her less confident but more deliberate strategy survive over Joe? Check the appropriate box below and compare your decision with that of the author on page 55.

☐ Joe will survive.

☐ Mary will survive.

☐ Both Joe and Mary will survive.

THE CHALLENGE AHEAD

Supervision is a special challenge that can help you reach new career and lifestyle goals. But becoming a successful manager is not as easy as some people imagine. Three factors will require that you be a "different" kind of person on the job.

1. Those in your department will expect you to lead where in the past you have been, like them, a follower. This means they will be watching your actions in the hope that you will make quick and good decisions that will lead the department in the direction that is best for the organization.

2. Your new role will put you in the position of being a "buffer" between your superiors and those you supervise. This means you must satisfy your superiors and, at the same time, keep your employees happy so they will maintain high productivity. At times this may mean it is best for you to absorb pressure from above rather than pass it on to your employees.

3. You will be setting standards rather than living up to those set by others. This means you will be responsible for creating a disciplined environment where employees do not violate company standards as well as those set by you. When violations occur, some sensitive counseling on your part may be necessary.

All of this should be accepted as a challenge that will help you go grow into a stronger person. And, of course, there are special rewards as listed on the next page.

WHAT CAN SUCCESS AS A SUPERVISOR DO FOR YOU?

Many good things can happen to you once you become a successful supervisor. Ten statements are listed below. *Three are false.* Place a check in the square opposite these false statements and match your answers with those at the bottom of the page.

As a supervisor you will:

☐ 1. Increase your earnings potential.

☐ 2. Have opportunities to learn more.

☐ 3. Develop an ulcer.

☐ 4. Position yourself for promotions to higher management.

☐ 5. Have less freedom.

☐ 6. Increase your self-confidence.

☐ 7. Try out your leadership wings.

☐ 8. Have fewer friends.

☐ 9. Learn and develop human relations skills.

☐ 10. Have better feelings of self worth.

You will find the *answers* to this exercise at the bottom of the page.

FALSE STATEMENTS

3. There is no evidence that supervisors have more ulcers than non-supervisors.

5. Supervisors normally have more freedom because they control their actions more than employees.

8. Good supervisors develop new friends (fellow supervisors) and keep many old ones.

Attitude is the way you look at things *mentally.* You have the power to look at your new position in any way you wish. If you look at it in a positive, enthusiastic manner you will communicate to your employees that you are *ready* to accept your new responsibility and they will enjoy working for you. If you are tentative or insecure they may interpret your attitude as negative and you may receive less cooperation.

As a new supervisor, everyone will be watching you and no matter what you may do to hide it, your attitude will be showing.

YOUR ATTITUDE* TOWARD BEING A SUPERVISOR

To measure your attitude, please complete this exercise. Read the statement and circle the number where you feel you belong. If you circle a 5, you are saying your attitude could not be better in this area; if you circle a 1, you are saying supervision may not be for you.

	Agree				Disagree
I seek responsibility.	5	4	3	2	1
Becoming a respected supervisor is important to me.	5	4	3	2	1
I enjoy helping others do a good job.	5	4	3	2	1
I want to know more about human behavior.	5	4	3	2	1
I want to climb the management ladder.	5	4	3	2	1
I am anxious to learn and master supervisory skills.	5	4	3	2	1
I like leadership situations.	5	4	3	2	1
Working with a problem employee would be an interesting challenge.	5	4	3	2	1
I intend to devote time to learn motivational skills.	5	4	3	2	1
I'm excited about the opportunity to become a supervisor.	5	4	3	2	1

TOTAL

If you scored above 40, you have an excellent attitude toward becoming a supervisor. If you rated yourself between 25 and 40, it would appear you have a few reservations. A rating under 25 indicates you probably should not pursue becoming a supervisor.

*For an excellent book on attitude, order *ATTITUDE: YOUR MOST PRICELESS POSSESSION* from page 58.

ATTITUDE AND PRODUCTIVITY

Nothing will improve relationships with those you supervise more than a consistently positive attitude on your part. Your attitude sets the pace and the tone in your department. If you are late to work, it will be reflected in the attitudes of your employees. If you complain about work conditions, it will impact in a negative way on their attitudes. Everything you do and every position you take will be reflected in the attitudes of your employees. Two expressions are appropriate. They are:

1. **ATTITUDES ARE CAUGHT, NOT TAUGHT!**

2. **YOUR ATTITUDE SPEAKS SO LOUDLY EMPLOYEES CAN'T HEAR WHAT YOU SAY.**

There is a direct relationship between your attitude and the productivity of those you supervise. When you are upbeat, your employees will respond in positive ways that will enhance productivity. When you are negative, a drop in productivity can be expected.

PRODUCTIVITY GAPS

In the diagram below, you will notice that there is a gap between what a hypothetical department is producing and what it *could* produce. We call this a departmental productivity gap. You will also notice there is a gap between what the employees are producing and what they could produce. Such gaps are normal and to be expected.

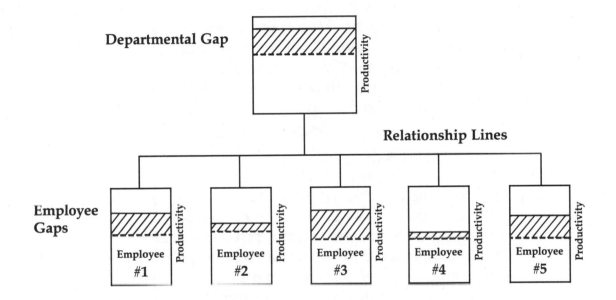

So how do you close the departmental productivity gap? The answer is to build such good relationships with your employees that they are motivated to close their individual productivity gaps. Of course, as a working supervisor, what you produce yourself is important. But it is the sum total of all producers that narrows the departmental gap. Not what you can do yourself.

All successful managers will tell you that it is what others produce for you that makes the difference. It is a lesson some beginning supervisors fail to learn.

Along with a positive attitude, it takes personal confidence to become a successful supervisor. When you first start out, you may not have *all* the confidence you would like, *but do not lose faith in yourself.* As a supervisor, you will slowly build your level of personal confidence. That is one of the advantages in becoming a supervisor in the first place.

As you accomplish this goal, keep in mind that you need not be a highly verbal extrovert to be successful. Quiet, sensitive people become excellent supervisors even though they may not show their personal confidence on the outside.

You have the "Right Stuff" or your superiors would not have given you the opportunity to become a supervisor in the first place. In management circles, the 'potted plant' theory is often expressed. Sometimes. Like a plant that is root-bound in a pot that is too small to permit growth, an employee often out-grows his or her position and only through a promotion into greater responsibilities (larger pot) can growth continue. This may be the best way to view your move into a supervisory role.

SELF-CONFIDENCE SCALE

This exercise is designed to help you discover your level of self-confidence. Read the statement and circle the number where you feel you belong.

	Agree				Disagree
I'm not easily intimidated.	5	4	3	2	1
Complex problems do not overwhelm me.	5	4	3	2	1
If necessary, I can discipline those who require it.	5	4	3	2	1
I can make a decision and stick with it.	5	4	3	2	1
I am strong enough to defend a deserving employee with a superior.	5	4	3	2	1
I have enough confidence to be a good teacher.	5	4	3	2	1
Speaking in public does not frighten me.	5	4	3	2	1
Superiors are basically people like me.	5	4	3	2	1
I won't avoid confrontations, when required.	5	4	3	2	1
I can say "no" when necessary.	5	4	3	2	1

TOTAL

If you scored 40 or above on both attitude and self-confidence, you have a winning combination as far as being a successful supervisor is concerned. If you scored lower on self-confidence than attitude, it is a signal that you need to learn to take a firmer stand on those items relating to supervision.

Supervisors are "in-charge" people. As leaders, they utilize their sources of power in sensitive but effective ways. When you assume your role as a supervisor-leader, you have three sources of power from which to tap.

First, you have "knowledge power" because of what you know about the department you lead. In most cases, you *know more* than those who work for you. When you teach them what you know, you make the best use of your "knowledge power."

Second, you gain power from the role you occupy. Just being the supervisor gives you authority which you must use gently and wisely.

Third, you have "personality power." You can persuade or motivate others through your positive attitude, friendly manner, patience and other personal characteristics.

Although you must be sensitive in the way you use your power (do not let your new position go to your head), properly used the three sources of power can help you become the kind of supervisor you want to be.

VITAL MESSAGE AHEAD

CONVERT TO A STRONGER IMAGE

It is important that a new supervisor learns to communicate a "take charge" image. She or he must let everyone know (co-workers and superiors) that things are under control—that decisions are being made and that the role of supervisor is comfortable. All of this must be accomplished without giving an impression that the new position has gone to the individual's head. It must be a natural transition.

Why is a stronger image necessary? Among other reasons, your employees want you to be a leader. They will produce more if they know they are part of a cohesive group with established standards. In contrast, a "weak" supervisor will cause employees to be confused and unproductive.

How do you communicate a stronger image? Here are some suggestions. Place a check in the square if you agree.

☐ *Improve your appearance.* Don't over-do it but look the part. Dress for success.

☐ *Make decisive decisions.* In making decisions, do it with confidence. Demonstrate you can handle decision-making.

☐ *Set a faster tempo.* Move about with more energy. Become a model of productivity.

☐ *Handle mistakes calmly.* When things go wrong, collect the facts, and develop a solution. Show your inner strength.

☐ *Share humorous incidents.* Balance your authority with a sense of humor. Help everyone have a little fun.

☐ *Demonstrate your ability to communicate with superiors.* Employees will feel more secure, and produce more when they know you can represent them with superiors.

☐ *Be a positive person.* Stay in touch with members of your crew in a positive manner. Keep in mind that their positive attitudes are dependent upon yours.

BECOMING A GOOD SUPERVISOR IS LIKE PLAYING BASEBALL

In baseball you must cover all four bases before you score a run and contribute to the success of the team. As a supervisor, there are four principles or foundations you must master to become effective and contribute to the productivity of your organization.

You must constantly remind yourself that you are the key player and those who work for you are counting on your support.

You need not be a baseball fan for the analogy to make sense.

YOU ARE UP TO BAT

COVER ALL THE BASES AND SUCCEED

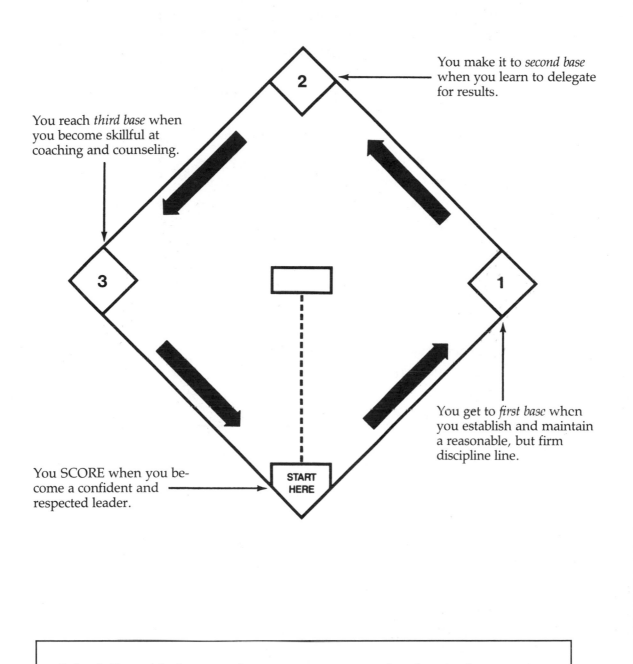

You make it to *second base* when you learn to delegate for results.

You reach *third base* when you become skillful at coaching and counseling.

You get to *first base* when you establish and maintain a reasonable, but firm discipline line.

You SCORE when you become a confident and respected leader.

In baseball you win the game when you score more runs than the opposing team. As a supervisor, you win the game when you get greater productivity from your players.

Establishing and maintaining fair, open, and healthy relationships with all employees is the key to good supervision. This includes the establishment of an authority or *discipline line*. This line is a well-defined, well-communicated set of behavior standards that you expect all employees to maintain. It tells an employee what is expected and what is not permitted.

Most employees enjoy working in an environment that has high but achievable standards. They feel more secure about their jobs when their supervisor is an "in-charge person" who does not permit one employee to "get by" with recognized violations.

It is important to set a reasonable and *consistent* discipline line. As you learn to do this, keep in mind that there is nothing incompatible about showing compassion and maintaining high standards at the same time.

TIPS ON GETTING TO FIRST BASE

DEMONSTRATE YOUR AUTHORITY AND STYLE

To reach first base you must demonstrate you are in charge and know what you are doing. You need to establish a style of your own. As you do this, give your team time to adjust. You are more interested in long-term, sustainable productivity than immediate results that may not last. This means the establishment of a sound working relationship with your employees.

In making your transition, consider these tips.

1. Set high (but attainable) standards at the outset. The lower your standards at the beginning, the more difficult it will be to improve productivity later.

2. Make an effort to etablish a good relationship with each employee on an individual basis as soon as practicable. This means working to get to know each employee personally and letting them know you care. It is not a sign of weakness to show understanding. You can be a sensitive supervisor and still be ''tough.''

3. Quickly counsel those who are not meeting your standards, so they have no doubts about what is expected.

4. Keep in mind that a few important standards (or rules) are better than a list of complicated directions. Do not be a ''picky'' supervisor. Instead, set basic terms that all understand and can attain.

Nothing undermines your authority faster than playing favorites. Employees need to be treated equally — especially if some are personal friends.

SETTING THE <u>RIGHT</u> DISCIPLINE LINE

As you become a supervisor you must draw a discipline line employees understand. The establishment of a values framework will allow your employees to operate securely. Supervisors must set discipline lines based upon their own, special work environment and individual style.

CASE 2

WHICH STRATEGY SHOULD HENRY USE?

Although sensitive to the needs of fellow-workers, Henry has always set higher standards for himself. He is never late, seldom absent and, once on the job, all business. Henry attributes his work style to his upbringing and religious training. Henry is respected more by management than fellow employees.

Yesterday Henry was promoted to become supervisor of his own department. When informed of the promotion, Henry's superiors told him: ''You were selected because we think you can put some discipline back into the department. As you know, your department is a mess, but we think you can clean it up. It won't be easy, but we have faith in you, Henry.''

Last night Henry sat down and developed three different strategies to consider. Which one would you recommend Henry employ?

Strategy 1   Set a good example and give employees time to adjust to it.

Strategy 2   Call a departmental meeting and, in a low-key manner explain the mission you have been given by your superiors. Explain that the higher standards you will impose will not only protect their jobs in the future but will give them more pride in what they are doing now. Tell them you will be tough but fair.

Strategy 3   Do the same as strategy 2 but on an individual counseling basis. Call in each person and explain the changes that will be made and why.

Write out your answer below.

I would recommend that Henry employ strategy _____ for the following reasons.

_____

_____

_____

Compare your answer with that of the author on page 55.

YOU MAKE IT TO SECOND BASE WHEN YOU <u>DELEGATE</u>

Delegating is the assignment of tasks and responsibilities to help employees make their best contribution to the overall productivity of your department. When you delegate you become a teacher. You tell an employee how to perform a new task effectively, show how it is done, and then ask that he or she demonstrate the task has been learned. Delegating takes time, patience, and follow-up to insure it is done right.

A supervisor must learn how to evenly distribute tasks, tap the special creativity of each individual, and, when appropriate, rotate responsibilities among different employees. Proper delegation keeps employees motivated, increases productivity, and frees the supervisor to perform more important activities.

THE CONTRIBUTIONS OF OTHERS MAKE YOU A GOOD SUPERVISOR

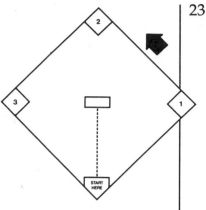

After setting a fair, consistent discipline line, the next big lesson is that you cannot do all the work yourself. You must delegate, and allow others to have responsibility to complete tasks which meet the expectations of your organization. This means that intelligent delegation is more important than the actual work you do yourself. Building good relationships with employees helps motivate them to do the work that needs to be done. It is great for employees to like you; but respect is more important. These tips will help you meet the challenge of getting to second base. Place a check in each square as you go through the list.

☐ Nothing builds respect better than demonstrating to employees that you know what you are doing. Knowledge gives you power, and when you share it, you earn respect. Teach those who work for you everything you know to help them become more efficient.

☐ Set a good example. It is smart to pitch in and work from time to time to demonstrate your compentency. But don't overdo it. Your skills are more valuable as a supervisor than a worker.

☐ Create a relaxed but efficient working climate. People make mistakes and produce less when supervision is too close and constant. People should be able to enjoy their work within your discipline line.

☐ Circulate and communicate. Give your employees every opportunity to do a good job and when they do, follow-up with compliments. Give credit freely when it is due.

☐ Keep an "open door" policy. That is, be accessible to employees. Welcome their suggestions and complaints. If you set a discipline line that is too "tight" you will destroy the environment employees need to produce at an optimum level.

When Molly was only twenty years of age, she became an instant supervisor without training. Although she was capable, enthusiastic, and did many things well, instead of delegating work Molly tried to do too much herself. As a result, she suffered burnout and decided that supervision was not "her bag." Later, at age twenty-five (after taking a course in beginning management), Molly had a second opportunity to be a supervisor. Realizing that she would be rated on what her employees did (productivity) more than what she did herself, she delegated as much as possible so she would have extra time to build good relationships, communicate, and plan. Today, at thirty-five, Molly is a successful vice president and still growing.

HOW TO DELEGATE

Quality delegation takes planning. You must analyze all of the tasks that need to be performed – before you start the process. Haphazard delegation can do as much harm as good.

HOW TO DELEGATE: STEPS TO TAKE

A supervisor who learns to delegate effectively achieves two goals at the same time. First, more time is available to plan, organize and maintain relationships with other employees and co-workers. Second, employees become more versatile and valuable as they learn new tasks.

Below are ten typical steps in the delegating process. As you check the list, assume you have been working extra hours and need to turn over tasks you have been doing.

☐ **Step 1**   Analyze your tasks and identify one you feel will provide you with additional freedom as well as benefiting the employee to whom you assign the responsibility.

☐ **Step 2**   Select the most logical individual for the task you identify and delegate it. Be careful not to overload one employee.

☐ **Step 3**   Instruct the individual selected how to perform the task. Do this in detail by both explaining and demonstrating. Explain why the task is important to the total operation.

☐ **Step 4**   Solicit feedback to insure the employee is prepared to assume the new responsibility. Provide opportunities for the employee to ask questions.

☐ **Step 5**   Allow the employee you selected the freedom to practice the new assignment for a few days. Over-supervision can kill motivation.

☐ **Step 6**   Follow up in a positive manner. When deserved, compliment the employee. If improvements are required, go through the instructional process a second time.

☐ **Step 7**   Consider the rotation of tasks. Done properly, employees learn more and boredom is less likely. Also, an objective productivity comparison is possible among employees.

☐ **Step 8**   Delegate those assignments which prepare employees to take over in the absence of others—including yourself.

☐ **Step 9**   Give everyone an opportunity to contribute. Solicit employee ideas. Utilize their special talents and abilities.

☐ **Step 10**   Discuss new assignments and rotation plans with the entire group to obtain feedback and generate enthusiasm.

If you are a sports fan, you know the primary job of a coach is to build a cohesive team. When everyone works together the team is more likely to win. Personality conflicts can destroy a team. They can also destroy productivity in a department. A supervisor is a coach. She or he must keep harmony among workers to insure productivity and win the game. The best way to do this is through good communciation and counseling.

GETTING TO THIRD BASE

Counseling is sitting down in a private setting for an open discussion with an employee. Sometimes it is to pay a sincere compliment; sometimes it is to solve a problem that is hurting productivity; sometimes it is because an employee violated your discipline line and you need to talk about improvement in behavior. There are many counseling skills.* One of the most important ones is being a good listener. This will help you find the *real* problem, and then help the employee make a mutually rewarding decision. There is no magic to good counseling. Anyone can do it.

*See *Personal Counseling* by Richard L. Knowdell and Elwood N. Chapman. Order form on page 58.

BECOME AN EFFECTIVE COUNSELOR

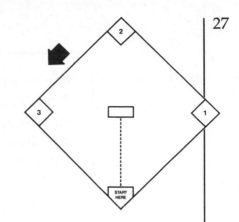

We communicate on several levels from individual to large groups. We also communicate both formally and informally. When you become a supervisor, communication of all types, at all levels takes on new importance.

Communicating one to one, in private, is called counseling or interviewing. Once you become a supervisor you will discover counseling is one of the best "tools" you possess. Until you understand what counseling can do for you, it will be difficult to get to third base.

Below are ten situations. Seven call for counseling by the supervisor. *Three do not*. Check the three that require no counseling. Check your answers with those given at the bottom of the page.

☐   1. When an employee violates your standards.

☐   2. When an employee is consistently late or absent.

☐   3. When you disagree with an employee's lifestyle.

☐   4. When an employee's productivity is down.

☐   5. When one employee behaves in such a way that the productivity of others is negatively affected.

☐   6. When you are upset.

☐   7. When two employees have a conflict that is becoming public.

☐   8. When you dislike the personality of an employee.

☐   9. When you want to compliment an individual.

☐ 10. When you want to delegate a new task.

> **If productivity drops in a department, action needs be taken quickly. Time normally will not solve problems that need to be addressed. Often action can take the form of counseling—either individual or group, or both.**

It is important to remember that individuals who become good first-line supervisors become candidates for middle and upper management positions. Those who demonstrate their skills in the minor leagues (supervision) are often promoted to the major leagues. In supervision, as in baseball, it is extremely important to get started on the right foot. If you weave the strategies and techniques of this book into your behavior patterns, you will be preparing yourself for a higher-paying, more challenging management role. Do not make the mistake of saying to yourself that excellent supervision is simply common sense. It is much more than that. That is why you should regularly review the skills you are learning so that you know and practice all of the competencies required to win the management game.

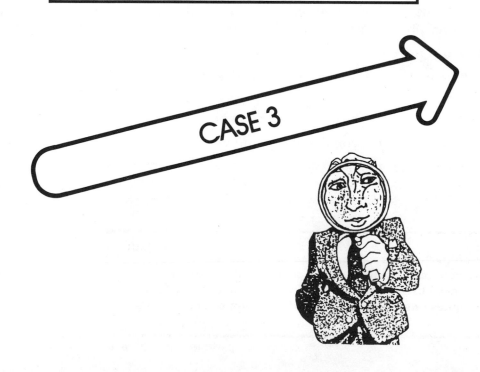

CASE 3

CAN SYLVIA KEEP HER JOB AS A SUPERVISOR?

Sylvia, without sensing it, has been spending too much time on budget and administrative reports and not enough time communicating with her ten employees. As a result, morale is low, productivity is down and two good employees are thinking about submitting their resignations. Everyone feels frustrated and unappreciated. The situation is so bad that Sylvia's boss called her into his office and informed her: ''Sylvia, you have committed a cardinal sin by neglecting your employees in favor of other responsibilities. Instead of delegating some of your work in order to free yourself, you locked yourself into your office and allowed things to fall apart outside. You could have great potential as a manager, but not until you learn to balance people activities with job tasks. You cannot have high productivity with low communication. All of your employees feel you have been taking them for granted. A few have even talked to me about it. Your job as supervisor is in jeopardy. Be in my office at ten o'clock tomorrow with a plan to restore morale and productivity within ten days.''

What are Sylvia's chances of coming up with a plan that will turn things around?

Please check the appropriate box below and write out the reasons for your choice.

☐	☐	☐	☐
Excellent	Good	Long Shot	Too Late

_____

_____

_____

Turn to page 55 to compare your answer with that of the author.

To be highly effective as a supervisor you will want to put more leadership into your style. Everyone likes to work for a supervisor who keeps them motivated and headed in the right direction. Just like baseball players build loyalty toward coaches that lead them to victory, employees like supervisors who lead them to greater achievements.

Leadership means stepping out in front of others with new, workable ideas that save money and create greater productivity. Leadership means creating *followers* – employees who respect you to the point they would like to follow you when you earn your next promotion. Becoming a supervisor is the best possible way to learn and practice leadership skills.

GETTING HOME SAFELY

BECOME A
GOOD LEADER

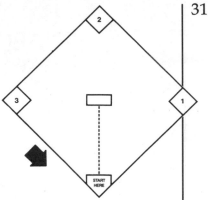

Your job as a supervisor is to establish departmental
goals and then lead your people to achieve them.
Keeping good records and insuring that everyone stays
busy is more management than leadership. Another
way of saying it is that managing is the protection of
what is already in place. Leadership, on the other hand,
is reaching for new heights. Managers keep things the way they are to
avoid trouble. Leaders take prudent risks to gain greater productivity.
YOU WANT TO BE A GOOD MANAGER, BUT YOU ALSO WANT TO
BE A LEADER.

To become both—and get home safely—consider these tips:

First, be a good manager. Insure your operation is conforming
to your organization's standards. Watch details. Get reports in on
time. Achieve the good feeling that comes from having everything
under control.

Next, become a positive influence. Set new goals and
motivate others to reach them. Stay positive. Keep things stirred
up. Don't permit employees to become bored.

Help your people reach their goals. Help them feel better
about themselves. Provide the rewards and recognition they
deserve. The better they feel about themselves, the more they will
produce.

Now and then establish your authority. Employees need to be
reminded that a discipline line exists. One way to demonstrate
your authority is to make decisive, difficult decisions. Another is
to counsel disruptive employees and expect continued
improvements in productivity.

Share good news. Keep the bad news in perspective. Look for
positive things to talk about, including individual and group
achievements. Make everyone feel that they are on a winning
team.

ESTABLISH A PRODUCTIVITY GOAL

Management By Objectives is a system whereby supervisors submit their goals to higher management, to be integrated with the organization's goals. Supervisors are rewarded when their goals are achieved or surpassed.

Your organization may not use this approach. If it does not; create your own goals (plans) on a weekly, monthly, and annual basis.

Those who set goals are usually more motivated to reach them. Even if management does not know about your goals (and does not hold you accountable for reaching them) you will benefit from having them.

GOALS AHEAD

Most people are goal-oriented. They like to be headed in a positive direction that will provide satisfaction.

PROVIDE DIRECTION!

Everybody likes to be on a winning team. In your organization, your department is a team which can win only if it reaches predetermined goals. IT IS YOUR RESPONSIBILITY AS SUPERVISOR TO HELP ESTABLISH SUCH GOALS AND THEN MOTIVATE YOUR PEOPLE TO REACH THEM.

Following are ten suggestions on how to motivate employees to reach a goal. Three are unacceptable because they will probably do more harm than good. Place a check in the squares opposite those that are counter-productive, and then compare your answers with those below.

☐ 1. Involve employees in the goal-setting process.

☐ 2. Make it easy for employees to motivate themselves by creating a relaxed and predictable working climate.

☐ 3. At meetings, lay down the law. Tell everyone you are the boss, and things are to be done your way.

☐ 4. Give employees credit when it is earned.

☐ 5. Circulate regularly and listen in order to discover the kind of rewards you can provide to improve productivity.

☐ 6. Act disappointed with everyone's performance as a method to get people to work harder.

☐ 7. Ask for suggestions from employees on how productivity can be improved.

☐ 8. Tell everyone that unless productivity improves their jobs are on the line.

☐ 9. Have a positive counseling session with each employee on a regular basis. Listen to complaints; and, when possible, make adjustments to resolve the issue.

☐ 10. Through your own positive attitude create a more lively and happy work environment.

> **It is important that each member of a team share in success. Communication is the only way this can happen.**

Answers to exercise 3, 6, 8

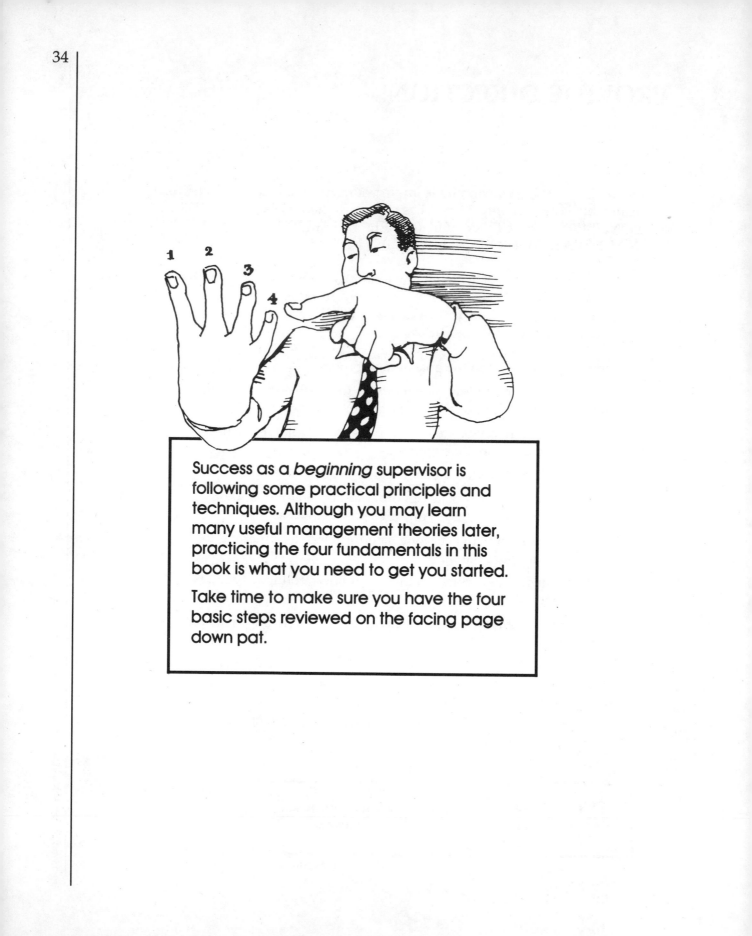

34

Success as a *beginning* supervisor is following some practical principles and techniques. Although you may learn many useful management theories later, practicing the four fundamentals in this book is what you need to get you started.

Take time to make sure you have the four basic steps reviewed on the facing page down pat.

PROVE YOU ARE READY TO BECOME A SUCCESSFUL SUPERVISOR

In the weeks ahead, keep the comparison between baseball and good supervision in your mind. Make a serious attempt to weave all four foundations (bases) into your style. To help you do this, please write the missing word in each of the following sentences.

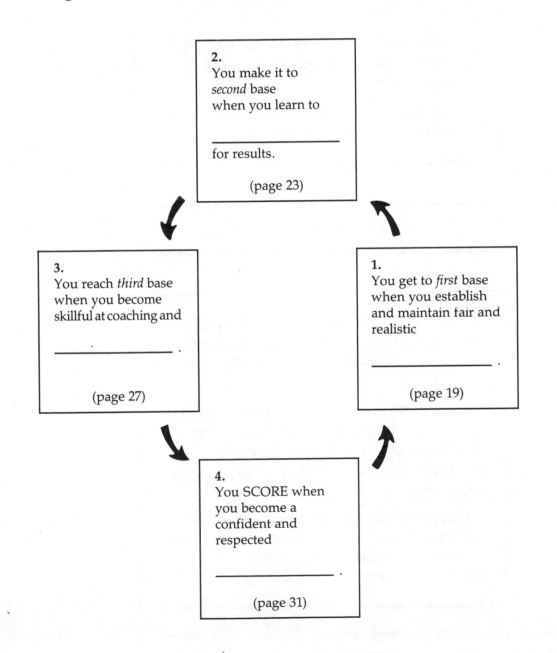

2.
You make it to *second* base when you learn to

_____

for results.

(page 23)

3.
You reach *third* base when you become skillful at coaching and

_____ .

(page 27)

1.
You get to *first* base when you establish and maintain fair and realistic

_____ .

(page 19)

4.
You SCORE when you become a confident and respected

_____ .

(page 31)

Gilbert is an outstanding producer, but he has a short fuse that often gets him into trouble. Maria is an excellent member of the department, but now and then she has a down period that requires great tolerance from her supervisor and co-workers. Cray makes a "buddy" out of all of his co-workers but becomes upset when they prefer to not include him in their activities.

Q. With such characteristics can Gilbert, Maria and Cray become successful supervisors?

A. Yes, but only if they can break those habits described above.

DANGER AHEAD

It is possible to tolerate such behavior as an employee but it could spell disaster should the same behavior surface as a supervisor.

After you hold down your job as supervisor for about three months, you will start to feel comfortable with your new role. However, you may need to change some habits before this happens.

If you are prone to make any of the mistakes listed on the following page, start to make corrections immediately or you will have trouble as a supervisor.

SIX UNFORGIVABLE MISTAKES

1. Treating individuals unequally because of sex, culture, age, educational background, etc. Each employee is unique and should receive the same consideration as any other.

2. Not keeping a trust with an employee. The fastest way to destroy a relationship is to make a promise and then break it.

3. Blowing hot and cold. Consistency is essential when managing. If you are positive one day and down the next, employees will not know how to react. Respect will disappear.

4. Failure to follow basic company policies and procedures. As a first-line supervisor, you must handle your relationship with each employee in a fair and legal manner. This may mean, for example, establishment of an ''improvement plan'' before you ask for approval to terminate an employee.

5. Losing your cool in front of others. Everyone reaches his/her threshold of tolerance on occasion; but, as a supervisor, your need to keep your temper in check. Blowing up can destroy relationships.

6. Engaging in a personal relationship with someone you supervise. When you become a supervisor, you change your role. It is poor policy to be in charge of a person during the day and personally involved with them after work.

In as few words as possible, write the six unforgivable mistakes, in your language, in the spaces below.

1. _____

2. _____

3. _____

4. _____

5. _____

6. _____

ELIMINATING PERSONAL DOWN PERIODS

It is not always easy to be positive. The responsibilities are often great and they can, without realizing it, turn you negative. The truth is, that when you are positive, productivity is up; but when you become negative, productivity drops. So your challenge is to remain positive even if those around you are not.

The exercise below assumes three things: (1) You are generally a positive, upbeat person. (2) There are certain things you can do to remain positive. (3) Being aware of these activities will assist you in the elimination of "down periods". After reading the list select the three that will do the most for you.

☐ Engage in physical exercise of some sort.

☐ Give yourself more attainable goals.

☐ Try to take life less seriously.

☐ Share your positive attitude with others.

☐ Take more week-end or "mini" vacations.

☐ Maintain a better balance between work and leisure.

☐ Improve your grooming.

☐ Do more to help others.

☐ Talk with a more experienced manager you respect to learn a solution to eliminate down periods.

Others:

_____

_____

_____

TRANSITION TIPS

- Stay warm and friendly but slowly back away. You can't be a "buddy" and a supervisor at the same time.

- Do not permit those who were co-workers yesterday to intimidate you today. If you play favorites you are in trouble.

- Do what you can to make everyone's job better than before you became supervisor. Do not make the same mistakes your boss made when you were an employee.

- Demonstrate to your previous co-workers that you are knowledgeable by teaching them in a sensitive manner new skills that will make their jobs easier.

- Seek more assistance from your superior in making your transition. Ask for suggestions. Be a good listener.

- Give previous co-workers credit when due.

PROVIDE REINFORCEMENT

Employees like to know how they are doing. Take a few minutes every now and then to let your people know you appreciate their dependability and the contribution they are making. Many capable employees resign because superiors take them for granted.

You are only as good as the people who work for you. Make sure your employees regularly receive the reinforcement they need.

All supervisors must occasionally deal with a difficult or "problem" employee. Some employees are consistently late or absent from work – others create false rumors that impact on the productivity of workers – still others fail to follow safety rules or make mistakes that need to be corrected. In extreme cases, problem employees carry hostility toward another employee or his or her supervisor.

How you deal with such employees and convert them into "team members" is a critical part of your job. The suggestions on the following pages are designed to provide you with the help you may need.

THE PROBLEM EMPLOYEE

REACTING TO THE PROBLEM EMPLOYEE

Below are ten ways to react to an employee who is demanding, hostile and disruptive. *Three are acceptable forms of behavior.* Place check in the box opposite those you feel are appropriate behavior for a supervisor. Then match your answers with those at the bottom of the page. Remember, we are talking about your intial reaction—not action that might be taken later.

☐   1. Stay cool. Let the employee express anger without an immediate reaction on your part.

☐   2. Let the employee know that you consider him or her to be a problem.

☐   3. Challenge the employee with a firm countenance.

☐   4. Consider the employee as objectively as possible and refuse to take things personally.

☐   5. Avoid the problem. Time will solve it.

☐   6. Become distant and non-communicative.

☐   7. Challenge the employee to stop giving you a problem.

☐   8. Act uninterested and ignore the situation.

☐   9. Get angry and give back the kind of behavior your receive.

☐ 10. In a calm manner say: "Let's talk in my office."

> Firm, friendly, and fair are the key words in maintaining your discipline line. But when a difficult situation arises, it is time to use your counseling skills.

Answers to exercise 1, 4, 10

To be an effective supervisor you need to know how to *create* and maintain relationships with members of your staff. Good relationships are created when you:

- Provide clear, complete instructions.

- Let employees know how they are doing.

- Give credit when credit is due.

- Involve people in decisions.

- Remain accessible.

THE BEST WAY TO MAINTAIN A RELATIONSHIP IS THROUGH FREQUENT COMMUNICATIONS.

CASE 4

WILL MRT COUNSELING WORK?

Kathy learned about MRT counseling last week. As she understands it, the idea is to sit down with a problem employee and discuss rewards she can provide for that employee, as well as rewards that employee can provide for her. The technique is based on The Mutual Reward Theory (MRT) which states that a relationship between two people can be enhanced when there is a satisfactory exchange of rewards between them. When the exchange is considered balanced, both parties will come out ahead.

Kathy has been having trouble with George for over a month. In desperation, she decides to call him into her office and openly discuss the situation to see if the Mutual Reward Theory can be applied. Her hope is that she can give him what he wants in exchange for a better attitude on his part.

Kathy starts the counseling session by complimenting George on his consistent productivity and asking him to suggest any rewards she is not providing that are within her capacity to provide. She informs George that she will, in turn, suggest three rewards she would like to receive from him.

Here are George's suggestions:
1. More opportunity to learn.
2. More recognition.
3. Less supervision by Kathy.

Kathy in turn asks for the following:
1. Continued high productivity.
2. More cooperation with co-workers.
3. Less hostility toward herself.

George and Kathy spend thirty minutes discussing the rewards each wants and how the other could provide them. George admits that he could be more cooperative; Kathy admits that she can provide George more opportunity to learn and they discuss a number of ways this can be accomplished.

Will this kind of MRT counseling work for Kathy? Will it improve the relationship between Kathy and George on a permanent basis? Write your answer in the space below and compare with that of the author on page 54.

_____

_____

_____

SUMMARY

Throughout this book you have learned that becoming a successful supervisor is a combination of many personal characteristics (positive attitude, personal confidence, patience, etc.) and the application of many tested skills and techniques (delegating, counseling, restoring relationships, etc.).

CAN YOU PUT ALL OF THESE REQUIREMENTS TOGETHER?

Of course you can – especially if you don't try to do everything at once! Keep in mind that after all is said and done, the key to your success as a supervisor is how well you achieve improved productivity.

If your department is regularly recognized for higher productivity than similar departments, your superiors will recognize this and you will be in a good position for future advancement.

Achieving greater productivity is a *human challenge.* As a supervisor, it is not what you can accomplish by doing tasks yourself but the quality of the working relationships you build with the employees *who do the work for you.*

HOW TO ACHIEVE GREATER PRODUCTIVITY

DEVELOP YOUR HUMAN SKILLS

As an employee, your productivity was measured and compared with your co-workers. Your superior normally did this through some kind of formal appraisal. Your promotion may have depended on these appraisals.

When you become a supervisor, you are measured by the productivity of your department or section. This means your future depends on how well your crew performs. If you employ the human skills which motivate your staff to produce more, you will be recognized for doing a good job. If the opposite happens, your job may be in jeopardy.

It helps to contribute to productivity by doing a small amount of work yourself. This, also, helps to set the work pace. If you do too much yourself, however, your people may not get the supervision which will allow them to produce more.

To test your understanding, please answer the following true and false questions. The correct answers are given below.

True   False

_____ _____   1. Nothing should receive higher priority than helping an employee reach his or her productivity potential.

_____ _____   2. A drop in productivity by a reliable employee need not be dealt with immediately as it might cause resentment.

_____ _____   3. Employees will often produce more for one supervisor than for another.

_____ _____   4. A disruptive employee who reduces the productivity of co-workers must be dealt with immediately.

_____ _____   5. Some employees with modest personal productivity can help the productivity of others so much that they are highly regarded by supervisors.

_____ _____   6. Most employees have higher productivity potential than they realize.

_____ _____   7. Generally speaking, the more employees produce, the better they feel about themselves.

_____ _____   8. Human skills are easier to learn than technical skills.

_____ _____   9. A think-smart supervisor can do less personally and still have the highest producing department.

_____ _____   10. A "golden" employee is one who produces at a high level and, also, contributes measurably to the productivity of co-workers.

Answers to exercise:
1. T, 2. F, 3. T, 4. T, 5. T, 6. T, 7. T, 8. F, 9. T, 10. T

KEEPING SUPERIORS HAPPY

When you become a supervisor it is not only keeping your employees happy and productive, it is also making sure that good relationships are maintained with your superiors. As mentioned earlier, you are the "buffer" and must be concerned with relationships in both directions.

Here are three suggestions to assist you in developing and maintaining a healthy, open relationship with *your* boss.

1. Tie your departmental goals to those of the firm as a whole. This means listening to changes that come down from above and bringing your section into line. Just as there are problem employees, there are problem supervisors. Don't be one.

2. Keep your superior informed. Share the good news (it is a good idea to have your superior compliment one of your deserving employees now and then) and openly admit any misjudgements you may have made.

3. Be a good team member. As a supervisor, you will need to build good relationships with supervisors and management personnel other than your immediate boss. In doing this, see that your superior is placed in the best possible light with others. Do this even though she or he may not give you all the recognition you feel you deserve.

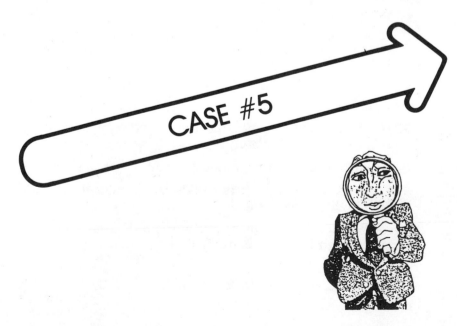

CASE #5

BETWEEN A ROCK
AND A HARD PLACE

Grace did so well as a beginning supervisor for her department store that they invited her to attend an all-day management workshop. When she showed up for work the following day her superior, Mr. Adams, called her into his office and questioned her harshly about the behavior of her employees. Knowing Grace was absent, Mr. Adams had dropped by her department at closing time and found her employees playing catch with some merchandise and laughing loudly. Grace, feeling let down by her staff, told Mr. Adams it would not happen again and on the following day came down hard on everyone at an informal staff meeting. Then, after checking the sales figures, Grace discovered her group had such a great sales day, (an all time record in fact) that they were simply in a happy mood because of their success. Mr. Adams had misinterpreted their behavior.

How, in your opinion, should Grace handle the situation? Write out your answer below and compare with that of the author on page 55.

REPAIRING RELATIONSHIPS

In becoming a successful supervisor, you will make your share of human relations mistakes. This is inevitable because your people responsibilities will be different. You will be exploring new human relations territory.

If you permit these mistakes to go unattended you may turn out to be the victim. This can happen when employees become offended and cut back on their personal productivity, start rumors, etc. You did not intend to damage a relationship but you become the victim anyway. To avoid this you may wish to consider the following:

1. Apologize by saying you are still learning the ropes.

2. Engage in some personal counseling with the injured party so that they can get anything bothering them out in the open. Communication is not only the best way to restore a relationship, often it is the only way.

3. Without showing any favoritism do something ''special'' to send the injured employee a signal that you know you made a mistake and that it won't happen again.

> You can build your supervisory style around the formula on the next page. It contains all of the basic ingredients required for success. If you wish, you may tear or cut it out and paste it on your refrigerator or mirror as a reminder. It will help you become comfortable and secure in your new role.

SUCCESS FORMULA FOR SUPERVISORS

POSITIVE ATTITUDE

Having a Positive Attitude is far more important when you become a supervisor

STRONG DISCIPLINE

Employees want you to set a fair and reasonable discipline line—and then maintain it for all employees. They also want to be lead into higher ground.

HUMAN SKILLS

Your challenge is to help those who work for you to grow and prosper. To do this you must be sensitive to their needs and recognize there are certain human relations skills that need to be practiced.

ATTENTION TO DETAILS

A supervisor must keep things under control in order to lead. Reports to management and personnel must be on time; equipment must be maintained; safety precautions must be honored; standards of cleanliness must be upheld. All of this should be accomplished without neglecting employees.

PREPARING FOR PHASE II

What you have learned from this booklet should be considered Phase I in an on-going plan of personal growth into higher management levels. Think of it as a strategy to get you off and running on the right foot. Later, perhaps sooner than you think, you may have the opportunity to attend a Phase II seminar offered by your organization. Or you can enroll in a management course at a local college on your own. One thing for certain, the progress you make in more sophisticated programs will depend upon your success with Phase I.

As you look ahead to your future in management, please keep the following in mind:

1. Nothing can take the place of a positive supervisory experience at the very beginning. Some individuals who get off to a bad start return to non-supervisory roles and never try again.

2. The more you apply the basic principles and simple techniques of this book the better your start will be.

3. Once you can handle the basics you will automatically become confident and insightful regarding more difficult management problems.

DEMONSTRATE YOUR PROGRESS

For each statement below, put a check under true or false.

True   *False*

_____ _____ 1. To make maximum use of this program you should review it regularly.

_____ _____ 2. *The Fifty Minute Supervisor* should be considered as Phase I of a more extended supervisory training program.

_____ _____ 3. One way to become a successful supervisor is to do more of the actual work yourself.

_____ _____ 4. Supervisors have less freedom than those they supervise.

_____ _____ 5. Behavioral changes are not necessary for most people to become good supervisors.

_____ _____ 6. Supervisors need not communicate a strong image.

_____ _____ 7. You get to first base when you establish and maintain a fair and consistant discipline line.

_____ _____ 8. Popularity is more important to the new supervisor than earning respect.

_____ _____ 9. In setting a discipline line, it is better to start easy and get tough later.

_____ _____ 10. It is easier to become a good supervisor when you are promoted within the same department.

_____ _____ 11. Most supervisors are good at delegating.

_____ _____ 12. Intelligent delegating takes too much time to be worthwhile.

_____ _____ 13. Supervisors should use counseling only as a last resort.

_____ _____ 14. Most supervisors are better at managing than leading.

_____ _____ 15. Supervisors who stay in the background and control with a firm hand are usually the most successful.

_____ _____ 16. Coaching and counseling are not important enough to be one of the four bases in the baseball analogy.

_____ _____ 17. Counseling is the best technique for working with a problem employee.

_____ _____ 18. Unlike employees, a supervisor does not have the luxury of reporting to work in a negative mood.

_____ _____ 19. Failure to keep a promise with an employee is not an unforgiveable mistake.

_____ _____ 20. Supervisors cannot afford to show compassion for employees.

[ ] **TOTAL**   **Turn page for answers.**

54

1. T Highly recommended.

2. T Hopefully you will be able to attend management seminars at a later date.

3. F A supervisor should *supervise*, not do actual work all the time.

4. F Supervisors have more freedom, especially if they learn how to delegate.

5. F Many behavioral changes are usually necessary.

6. F A stronger image is necessary but, of course, it should not be done too quickly or over-done.

7. T (See page 19)

8. F

9. F Just the opposite; start out with a firm but fair line and relax to the proper point later.

10. F Just the opposite.

11. F

12. F It takes time at the beginning but releases time in the future.

13. F Counseling is a tool that can be used daily.

14. T

15. F Constant communication through circulation is required.

16. F Coaching and counseling constitute third base.

17. T

18. T If the supervisor is down the entire crew may be.

19. F

20. F There is nothing incompatible about being compassionate and still maintaining a strong, productive discipline line.

AUTHOR'S SUGGESTED ANSWERS TO CASES

Who Will Survive? It is the opinion of the author that both Joe and Mary will survive, but the edge is with Mary. Joe will probably be better liked as a supervisor. Mary, however, will probably earn more respect. Joe ignores the fact that there are many sound techniques and principles every supervisor should learn. He will survive only if he learns them in time.

Which Strategy Should Henry Use? The author favors strategy 2 but would, also, follow up the group session with individual counseling to avoid any misunderstandings and improve relationships. Henry should not expect 100% compliance to his new standards quickly. He should, however, set his standards high enough to achieve the kind of productivity desired. Reachable standards are required, but employees should be given sufficient time to reach them. While doing this, Henry should, also, set a good example both as a supervisor and worker.

Can Sylvia Keep Her Job As A Supervisor? It is doubtful that Sylvia can turn things around. In fact, in similar situations, many experienced managers would transfer Sylvia to a non-supervisory position until she can demonstrate she is ready to assume the full responsibility of being a supervisor. Sylvia's boss is right in saying she committed a cardinal sin. The only way a supervisor can increase or maintain productivity is to establish and nuture good relationships with all employees. Once other activities take priority, morale begins to fall and trouble starts. Restoring relationships at this point is a long shot. Once relationships have deteriorated to a certain point, rebuilding them is almost impossible.

Will MRT Counseling Work? If both Kathy and George make a serious effort to provide one or more of the rewards wanted but not previously provided, the chances are excellent that the relationship will improve. MRT counseling frequently works because it opens up communication and both parties accept that there is something specific to do to make improvements. Care should be taken to announce in advance that there may be some rewards (like an increase in pay) over which the supervisor does not have jurisdiction or complete control.

Between A Rock and A Hard Place. First Grace should go to Mr. Adams and explain the reason for their behavior and stand up for them and their high productivity. Second, she should tell her staff what happened at the meeting with Mr. Adams. A supervisor's first responsibility is to go to bat for his or her staff.

ABOUT THE FIFTY-MINUTE SERIES

"Fifty-Minute books are the best new publishing idea in years. They are clear, practical, concise and affordable — perfect for today's world."

Leo Hauser
(Past President, ASTD)

What Is A Fifty-Minute Book?

—Fifty-Minute books are brief, soft-cover, "self-study" modules which cover a single concept. They are reasonably priced, and ideal for formal training programs, excellent for self-study and perfect for remote location training.

Why Are Fifty-Minute Books Unique?

—Because of their format and level. Designed to be "read with a pencil," the basics of a subject can be quickly grasped and applied through a series of hands-on activities, exercises and cases.

How Many Fifty-Minute Books Are There?

—Those listed on the facing page at this time, however, additional titles are in development. For more information write to **Crisp Publications, Inc., 95 First Street, Los Altos, CA 94022.**

Crisp books are distributed in Canada by Reid Publishing, Ltd., P.O. Box 7267, Oakville, Ontario, Canada L6J 6L6.

In Australia by Prime Learning Australia, Rochedale South, 7 Deputor Street, Brisbane, Queensland.

And in New Zealand by Prime Learning Pacific, 18 Gibbons Road, Weymouth, Auckland.

THE FIFTY-MINUTE SERIES

Quantity	Title	Code #	Price	Amount
	The Fifty-Minute Supervisor—*2nd Edition*	58-0	$6.95	
	Effective Performance Appraisals—*Revised*	11-4	$6.95	
	Successful Negotiation—*Revised*	09-2	$6.95	
	Quality Interviewing—*Revised*	13-0	$6.95	
	Team Building: An Exercise in Leadership—*Revised*	16-5	$7.95	
	Performance Contracts: The Key To Job Success—*Revised*	12-2	$6.95	
	Personal Time Management	22-X	$6.95	
	Effective Presentation Skills	24-6	$6.95	
	Better Business Writing	25-4	$6.95	
	Quality Customer Service	17-3	$6.95	
	Telephone Courtesy & Customer Service	18-1	$6.95	
	Restaurant Server's Guide To Quality Service—*Revised*	08-4	$6.95	
	Sales Training Basics—*Revised*	02-5	$6.95	
	Personal Counseling—*Revised*	14-9	$6.95	
	Balancing Home & Career	10-6	$6.95	
	Mental Fitness: A Guide To Emotional Health	15-7	$6.95	
	Attitude: Your Most Priceless Possession	21-1	$6.95	
	Preventing Job Burnout	23-8	$6.95	
	Successful Self-Management	26-2	$6.95	
	Personal Financial Fitness	20-3	$7.95	
	Job Performance and Chemical Dependency	27-0	$7.95	
	Career Discovery—*Revised*	07-6	$6.95	
	Study Skills Strategies—*Revised*	05-X	$6.95	
	I Got The Job!—*Revised*	59-9	$6.95	
	Effective Meetings Skills	33-5	$7.95	
	The Business of Listening	34-3	$6.95	
	Professional Sales Training	42-4	$7.95	
	Customer Satisfaction: The Other Half of Your Job	57-2	$7.95	
	Managing Disagreement Constructively	41-6	$7.95	
	Professional Excellence for Secretaries	52-1	$6.95	
	Starting A Small Business: A Resource Guide	44-0	$7.95	
	Developing Positive Assertiveness	38-6	$6.95	
	Writing Fitness-Practical Exercises for Better Business Writing	35-1	$7.95	
	An Honest Day's Work: Motivating Employees to Give Their Best	39-4	$6.95	
	Marketing Your Consulting & Professional Services	40-8	$7.95	
	Time Management On The Telephone	53-X	$6.95	
	Training Managers to Train	43-2	$7.95	
	New Employee Orientation	46-7	$6.95	
	The Art of Communicating: Achieving Impact in Business	45-9	$7.95	
	Technical Presentation Skills	55-6	$7.95	
	Plan B: Protecting Your Career from the Winds of Change	48-3	$7.95	
	A Guide To Affirmative Action	54-8	$7.95	
	Memory Skills in Business	56-4	$6.95	

(Continued on next page)

THE FIFTY-MINUTE SERIES
(Continued)

☐ Send volume discount information.

☐ Add my name to CPI's mailing list.

	Amount
Total (from other side)	
Shipping ($1.50 first book, $.50 per title thereafter)	
California Residents add 7% tax	
Total	

Ship to: _____

_____

_____

_____

Phone number: _____

Bill to: _____

_____

_____

_____

P.O. # _____

All orders except those with a P.O.# must be prepaid.
Call (415) 949-4888 for more information.

BUSINESS REPLY
FIRST CLASS   PERMIT NO. 884   LOS ALTOS, CA

POSTAGE WILL BE PAID BY ADDRESSEE

Crisp Publications, Inc.
95 First Street
Los Altos, CA 94022

NO POSTAGE
NECESSARY
IF MAILED
IN THE
UNITED STATES

NOTES

NOTES

NOTES

NOTES

NOTES

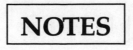

NOTES